How to Brand Yourself and Your Business

HOW TO BRAND YOURSELF & YOUR BUSINESS

*Proven Steps
to Building a Lasting
Universal Brand*

Daniel Ayodele

First published by Raedable 2021

How to Brand yourself and your Business

Copyright © 2021 by Daniel Ayodele

All rights reserved. No part of this publication may be reproduced, stored or transmitted in any form or by any means, electrical, mechanical, photocopying, recording, scanning, or otherwise without written permission from the author or publisher. It is illegal to copy this book, post it to a website, or distribute it by any other means without permission.

Daniel Ayodele asserts the moral rights to be identified as the author of this work.

This book was professionally typeset, designed and distributed online by Raedable.

Readable Publishing

House 3/5 Solomon Onafowope Street Abule Oshorun Ibeshe Ikorodu, Lagos, 104101 Raedable@gmail.com 2348124935612 / 2349018196749

Branding

Contents

Introduction vi

1 **Expand** the Brand — 1
2 **Contract** the Brand — 4
3 **Publicity** is a Good Thing — 7
4 **Advertising** the Brand — 10
5 Be **Authentic** — 14
6 It's not all about **Quality** — 17
7 **Category** over Brand — 20
8 The Importance of a **Name** — 23
9 Keep it **Simple** — 25
10 Don't be a **Stuck Up** Brand — 28
11 A second Thought on **Naming** — 31
12 Keep Brand Names and Company Names **separate** — 34
13 Beware of **Subbranding** — 37
14 Can You ever **Extend** the Brand — 40
15 The Importance of the **Logo** — 44
16 The Importance of **Colour** — 47
17 Think **Globaly** — 50

18 **Branding** and the Internet	53
19 **Naming** and the Internet	58
20 **Globalization** and the Internet	62

Conclusion 65

Introduction

When you think of a brand, the first thing that probably comes to your mind is the brand made on livestock. If so, you are on the right track as the branding of a product is not different in this sense. A successful brand sets your product apart from that of the competition and fulfils your desire for a brand that has the potential to expand your customer base while increasing your market share.

The larger your customer base and market share, the more powerful your brand. Yet, there are many factors that go into making a brand successful just as there are even more considerations to ensuring it stays successful. The basic steps you are about to learn are based on the concept that marketing and branding go hand in hand and they will enable you put your brand on the path to success. In essence, having a good brand will help your marketing and strong marketing will help you build a strong brand. However, it is up to you to do your homework in order to make the right decisions in the task of building such a brand.

In this quest, your goal should be to build a brand that is the recognized leader in a given category. This motivates consumers to align with your brand and makes them seek it out at the store for the satisfaction that they made the correct decision for themselves and their family when they patronized your brand.

With the explosion of the Internet, now more than ever, companies have the chance to go global and to increase their sales and profits. By following the steps outlined here – beyond having the information you need to make your brand successful – you will be able to take advantage of this opportunity to expand your reach both in the physical space and on the Internet as a brick-and-mortar store.

Daniel Ayodele

1

Expand the Brand

When you have a company that has products on the market, you have to decide if you want to expand the brand or maintain the status quo. If you do choose the former, there is a need to realize that expanding a brand can be a delicate decision since you do not want to do any harm to your brand by expanding too quickly.

Some companies decide to expand their brand quickly in order to benefit in the short term while others look for long-term success. To know how brand expansion can weaken your brand, you only have to study car manufacturers and the automobile industry. At one time, the three big automakers were untouchable. Consumers were proud to state that they drove a Ford, a Chevrolet, or a Chrysler. However, as the automakers introduced more and more models, their brands were weakened and consumers no longer stated that they drove a Ford, a Chevrolet, or a Chrysler; rather, they said they drove an Escort, a Cavalier, or a New Yorker. This shift from being brand-centered to becoming model-centered ultimately saturated the market, weakened their brand, and lessened their market share, allowing the competition the opportunity to move into their territory.

Does this mean that weakening a brand is a bad thing and might prevent your company from increasing profits? Far from it! If you are in an industry that has a weak or no competition, weakening your brand through expansion will open it up to the possibility of a larger market share, allowing you to increase sales and to make a larger profit.

On the other hand, you have to keep in mind the consumers who want to buy your product or identify with your brand. Having a brand that is everywhere and open to everyone might not be what the consumers are looking for. Think about the exclusivity of some brands like Rolex; not everyone can afford a Rolex watch, but the brand remains strong and retains the loyalty of those consumers who can afford it for that very reason. Being exclusive does have its benefits as much as being available to the population at large.

Branding

2

Contract the Brand

Having a brand that is associated with doing one or just a few things well will help you build a strong brand. If you want to open a business, it is okay to sell just a few items. If you want to open a restaurant, focus on being great with just a few dishes. Think of all the specialty stores that are out there which specialize in selling one thing or focus on a particular genre. Toy stores, for example, fit into this niche. Although they sell a variety of products, they are all geared toward toys. Girls' toys, boys' toys, it does not matter. When you are going into a toy store, you know exactly what you are going to see and you know why you are there. This adds value to their brand, whether they are well-known toy stores such as Toys "R" Us, or just regular neighborhood toy stores.

The same goes for restaurants. If you want to open an Italian restaurant, do not include dishes that do not fit within the scope of your business. Focus on doing Italian dishes right and you will build a well-respected brand for doing it well. There are certain rules you should follow to ensure that your brand benefits if you want to specialize or contract:

First, make sure you keep whatever business you want to be involved in simple and narrow.

Second, keep the supply of your product full at all times.

Third, when dealing with wholesalers, strike the best possible price so you can sell your product at inexpensive prices.

Fourth, make sure that you are the best at whatever you choose so that being the leader in the industry will give you a good brand identity.

Think of the large companies in the world that dominate in their category by focusing on one product. Coca Cola, for example, is the worldwide leader by far when it comes to selling carbonated beverages. Recent studies have put the company's share of the worldwide market in the neighborhood of seventy percent. Pundits should not even refer to the perceived rivalry between Coca Cola and Pepsi as a cola war because there is a clear winner in their category. Same situation applies in the case of McDonald's and Burger King. They are successful because they focus on making hamburgers and on being good at just a few items, in spite of the fact that they have expanded their menus to include chicken.

3

Publicity is a Good Thing

If you are looking to get a new brand off the ground, perhaps the best way to go about it is to generate as much publicity as you can. While advertising is another option, publicity is much better at getting a new product or brand going since it is a lot cheaper compared to advertising. Think about what you want your brand to stand for; if it is something to be used by people who will spend time outdoors or is relatable to being outdoors, you can go around the country spreading the message of your new product at outdoor festivals and country fairs. Show up at outdoor sporting events such as the X-Games as well as action sports events, pass out fliers, and give out free samples of your product to start creating a buzz among potential consumers.

One great way to generate publicity for your brand is to be the first at something. News people love the breaking news and always want to be the first on the scene of a new story. With the news media now connected across the world, it will cost next to nothing to get them to break the news about your brand or product. They will practically do the job for you. Also, with the advent of social media platforms such as Facebook and Twitter, you can create your own buzz about your brand free of charge!

You should not worry about trying to come up with a catchy slogan for your brand when you are trying to launch it. Stay focused on building as much publicity for your brand as possible. This will cut down the initial costs of launching your new brand so you can use your budgeted funds in other areas that will help make the brand a success. When thinking of strategies to deploy in order to increase your brand awareness, do so with the intent to get the most publicity at the lowest possible cost.

Branding

4

Advertising the Brand

Once you have launched your brand through publicity, the next step is to keep the brand name in the minds of consumers. This is done through advertising. Advertising can be an expensive proposition so it has to be approached carefully and with a well thought out plan. The message that you put forth through advertising is important. You will have to figure out the image you want to portray for your company and brand. However, if you have successfully positioned your brand through publicity and have become a leader in your industry, the best way to advertise is to advertise why your brand is the best. You do this by building an advertising campaign around your brand as the best in your market or you build an advertising campaign about how your brand is the leader in quality when it comes to products in your market. Consumers want to be associated with the best so you will find that they are attracted to your brand when you advertise about how your brand is an industry leader.

In order to make your advertising campaign a success, it is best to do some research beforehand. Hold some surveys and focus groups to get consumer feedback on your product and to get an understanding of how it is perceived before you get started. By doing this, you will be better prepared to construct a message that will resonate with consumers and entice them to try your brand for the first time or keep them coming back for more as repeat customers.

When you have a successful brand, you should strive for your brand name to create the intended image or word in the minds of consumers when they hear it. For example, if you have a brand that caters to high-end clientele, the first thing you want coming to their minds when they hear the name of your brand is quality, or perhaps exclusivity. Once your brand has achieved this status, the sky is the limit. It will become the unmitigated leader in the marketplace and will drive out the competition for the very fact that it will cost them too much to break into the market. Nevertheless, an important note of warning is necessary at this point. When you become a word or image in the minds of consumers, do not get cocky and try to expand. This will undo all the work that you have put into becoming a successful brand.

Think again about successful brands in the marketplace right now. When consumers go out to a restaurant and ask for a soda to drink, what do they say? They say I will have a Coke. They do not say I want a Pepsi, or a RC. This shows the dominance that Coca Cola has in the market. The same can be said for copiers. When someone says they are going to use the copier machine, they say they are getting some Xerox copies. Nobody says that they are going to get some Kyocera copies. No matter what the machine they are using is, Xerox is the brand mentioned because when consumers hear the word copy, Xerox comes to mind. Again, when you have a cold and need to blow your nose. What do you ask for? Kleenex, right? No matter the brand of tissues that you have in your home, when the time comes to wipe your nose, you ask for a Kleenex – one more example of a brand being so dominant that its brand name becomes the generic word for all items that are in competition with it.

5

Be Authentic

Consumers are people and people are guarded by nature. Therefore, no matter how well you try to get your message across through advertising, consumers will naturally question some of the claims you make. This is why the claims that you make in your advertising message have to be true and verifiable. This will give your brand the credibility it needs to reassure consumers that it does what you say it does and that it is of the quality that the advertisement says it is. Once you have established this with consumers, they will be more apt to tell other consumers about your brand and about how it backs up its claims. This could very well lead to your expansion and guarantee higher revenues and profits for your brand in the marketplace. Remember, expanding in the marketplace is a good thing; it is not the same as expanding the brand.

Being authentic in your advertising and being able to back it up will help your brand maintain leadership in the marketplace. In addition, it can also bring you free publicity – as an industry leader with good brand recognition, media outlets will be more likely to come to your company to do a story about your industry – this allows your brand to become a spokesperson for the industry while giving it a platform to become more recognized. Consumers, seeing your brand being featured in a news story, will ascribe more credibility to it and thereby increase its chance of expanding in the marketplace.

Don't forget. Gaining leadership with your brand is the most important thing you can do as a business owner as companies and products whose brands are leaders in the market are difficult to replace. In fact, a recent study of companies that were leaders in the marketplace in the 1940s showed that, out of the twenty brands that were researched, only three are not in the leadership position today. Leadership means long-term success, so strive to be on top.

6

It's not all about Quality

That a brand or product has the best quality does not necessarily mean it is destined to be number one. There are many brands that can be referenced to make this point. Just because a consumer paid a lot more for their Tag Heuer wristwatch does not mean that it will work better or tell the time more accurately than a Seiko. Additionally, paying thousands of dollars more for a BMW over a Toyota does not mean that the BMW will have less mechanical problems than the Toyota. In the same vein, paying more for a designer T-shirt does not mean that it will have a longer wear time than a T-shirt purchased at a discount store. In almost every industry, being the leader in quality does not always translate to being the leader in sales.

The perception that your brand is of quality is what you want in the minds of consumers and you can make that happen by becoming a brand with a specialty in the market. If consumers see that your brand is focused on just one area or a problem, they will perceive it as having more knowledge about that problem and, as a result, judge it as being of more quality. Another way to make a brand have the perception of quality is to make it more expensive than the competition's. This gives the consumer the psychological contentment that they bought the best quality brand on account of the price tag and the brand's potential to speak to a consumer's status. Consumers do not simply buy a more expensive brand for themselves, they do so to show the people they come in contact with that they can afford it.

When offering your brand for a higher price than that of your competitors, it is best that the brand enters the market already priced higher. This gives the consumer the impression that your brand is superior to the others based on price alone. Introducing the brand at a competitive price and then raising it makes it look like you are trying to gouge consumers. However, when you do offer a brand at a higher price than your competitors, you must ensure that there is something that gives the brand an extra quality. It could be as simple as having better packaging than the competition, but something has to justify the higher price. Remember that having brand quality means that you have to specialize in a given marketplace so that your brand will have the most recognized name for which you can charge more.

Branding

7

Category over Brand

You have already read that by specializing in a market you will be able to increase brand awareness. Now, try to think even further. Narrow your focus until you are able to create your own category. This has happened many times in the business world. When Apple introduced the iPad, a new category was formed for handheld devices. The same can be said for Atari when they introduced the Atari 2600 – they put in motion a completely new category of home gaming that continues to thrive.

To create your own brand category, there are some steps you need to accomplish: First, when you bring the brand to the marketplace, do so in a way that makes it appear that yours is the first brand to do what it is you want to do. This gives your brand the perception of being the leading authority in this area. Second, it is up to you to advance this new category in the eyes of the consumer. It will be of greater benefit to your brand to promote the category and not the brand in this situation. Promoting the category will promote the brand at the same time.

When you have created the new category and it is successful, there will be competitors that will come racing into the marketplace trying to profit from your foresight. Do not concern yourself too much with them; do not try to diversify your brand to counteract their coming into your territory. Continue with what has worked for you and promote the category over your brand. By being first to get into the category, your brand will remain visible as the most knowledgeable with the best quality to offer and will dominate the marketplace. Go back to the example of the iPad. While other companies have entered the category, iPad is still the clear leader and more consumers choose to purchase it over its nearest competitors.

8

The Importance of a Name

Deciding what the name of your product will be might be the most important decision that you have to make when you plan to bring your brand to the market. In the long run, that is what branding comes down to – the name.

Having long-term stability is the most important attribute of a brand name. This is because, after the initial push to get your brand to the market and the inevitable appearance of competition, the name will be what sets your product apart from that of the latter.

This takes us back to the need for your brand to be the first in your chosen category as this confers on your brand name a higher recognition value than the competition's, giving it visibility as the leader and authority in the category. Where this is the case, consumers returning to the store will specifically look for your product and avoid that of your competitor.

When you are thinking of names for your brand, you need to take into account what the product does as well as the age range of the target market. Also, the name should be kept as straightforward as possible so that it is simple for consumers to remember. Stay away from names that could be perceived as negative; the name you choose should evoke something positive in the mind of consumers when they hear it or read it, motivating them to identify with your brand and your product. In the best case scenario, being seen as a quality product and brand will increase your product's market share, leading to more sales and greater profits.

9

Keep it Simple

Be focused on keeping your brand special and limited. The easiest way to devastate a brand is to broaden the product line too far.

More and more manufacturers are extending their product line and weakening their brands. However, not only does this weaken their brands, it also takes power away from the manufacturers and gives it to retailers. This is because retailers have a limited amount of shelf space and, with many manufacturers extending their product line, they can charge more money to the manufacturers for that space.

For a prime example of the above, visit your local supermarket and go to the aisle that sells beer. Is there really enough demand on the planet to have over five variations of Miller Beer? You would think that regular and light would do the trick. Having more varieties of the same brand of beer does not increase sales or consumption; it just leads to more production and distribution costs. As a consumer, how many times have you been in front of a shelf at the store looking for a specific product and found it difficult to make up your mind due to the availability of so many choices? Avoiding such situations is the whole point of keeping your brand focused and specialized.

When consumers see over five varieties of a product line of one brand but then see that there is just one of yours for the same purpose, they will conclude that your brand is not trying to be all things to all people and are more likely to choose yours. You have to avoid this pitfall of creating varieties of the same product with your brand. Many companies believe that when their initial brand do well it gives them carte blanche to expand their product line as quickly as possible in order to cash in. While this might boost sales and revenue in the short term, it will destroy your brand over the long haul because you have weakened it too much. Additionally, by expanding your product line, you weaken the first product that brought you success in the first place. This is not a winning proposition. Therefore, keep it simple and specialize and your brand will be successful for many years to come.

Branding

10

Don't Be A Stuck Up Brand

If your brand gets to the point of being a leader in the marketplace, do not be afraid of other companies getting into the market to give your brand some competition. In fact, it is good for brands that are leaders in their market to welcome the competition. One of the good things about competition is that consumers like to have the ability to choose a product. McDonald's would not be where they are today if it was not for Burger King and Wendy's. The same can be said for Coca Cola. The brand would not be the same without Pepsi. One more example would be pharmacies. How often do you drive down the street, see a Walgreens and then, no more than a block later, see a CVS? They are basically stores that offer the same products yet there they are right next to each other. It does not matter what town you are in, they are always next to each other. If there is no competition in your category, consumers may look at your brand with doubt and pass on the opportunity to purchase it. This is why competition is important.

When the competition does come, you have to fight against the impulse to expand your brand in order to protect your market share. However, you do not want too much competition. This is because too much competition equals too many choices which confuse consumers and actually decrease sales across the whole category. For this reason, it is good to have a few select competitors in the same category as your brand to ensure that the marketplace thrives. Do not forget that it behooves your brand to be the first in the category so it is seen as the leader. That way you get to maintain your dominance in the category while receiving help to stay as the leader because of the competition.

Daniel Ayodele

11

A Second Thought On Naming

As you previously read, coming up with a name for your product is perhaps the most important decision you will have to make in building a brand. There are some important factors to remember when you are choosing a name for your brand or product.

First of all, you do not want to give your brand or product an ordinary name. Stay away from naming your product or brand national this or general that. There are so many products and brands that start with "general" or "national" such that choosing such names will not give your product or brand the individuality it needs to leave a mark in the minds of consumers. When products have names that essentially sound generic, it hinders them from becoming the major brand in their category.

Second, pay more attention to how the name sounds over how it looks when it is written down. Consumers will more likely hear the name of your product or brand before they read about it. One of the most successful ways to name a product or brand is to use an everyday word and use it out of context. Take Best Buy for example. If the electronics store was only called "Best" or "Buy" it would not have the same impact on consumers as it does when they hear the words "Best Buy" which gives the consumer the notion that they are going to find what they are looking for in the store and at the best price. Besides, the name Best Buy is simple and easy to remember and it gives consumers a positive image in their head when it is mentioned.

Circuit City, on the other hand, did not fare so well with basically the same business. When a consumer hears the words "Circuit City", they might know what the brand sells and yet prefer to go to Best Buy to purchase the same product due to Circuit City's lack the positivity. Is the consumer going to get the best buy at Best Buy? Maybe, maybe not. But they will feel better about themselves and the purchase, in part due to the name of the store. Here is where not overextending the brand comes into play. As long as Best Buy continues to focus on electronics and home appliances, they should be able to maintain their place in the market. However, if you start to see Super Best Buy stores that include supermarkets popping up all over the place, they will soon be in trouble. It is one thing to go to a Super Walmart or Super Target for groceries but to do that at an electronics store would be too far out of the ordinary and the latter's place in the market would quickly disappear.

Branding

12

Keep Brand Names And Company Names Separate

Brand names should always take priority over the company name. When consumers go shopping, they go looking for brands and not for companies. Think about when you are at the supermarket. How many company names do you see on a product? Most likely, you do not even notice them, even though they might be there. As consumers, we have been well-trained to look for the brand name. If you decide to put your company name on a product, make sure that the font size is smaller than that of the brand name. Never forget that you are selling a brand first.

Furthermore, as the head of your company, it is important for you to remember that consumers do not see things the same way you do. While you have to try to make the company as successful as possible – and that is your main concern – consumers are more worried about the brand name. Nobody says they are going to the supermarket to buy some Procter & Gamble laundry soap. They say that they are going to buy Tide. However, to help build your brand, include the company name somewhere on the packaging.

A problem can arise if consumers start using both your company name and the brand name to identify your product. This is a failure of your branding strategy. For whatever reason, the brand name has not stuck with consumers and they are having a hard time figuring out what the message is that your company is trying to convey. For example, look at the success of home gaming systems. When you hear the brand name Playstation, you know two things right off the bat: It is a video game system and it is made by Sony. You never hear it mentioned in advertisements as a Sony Playstation. Sony has successfully put the brand name first and it has become recognized as a brand by consumers who also know that the product is made by Sony. This is demonstrated when consumers go to purchase the product. They do not ask the sales associate where the Sony Playstation is; they just say Playstation.

Conversely, Microsoft takes a different approach to branding when compared to Proctor & Gamble and Sony. Their company name is displayed prominently on the packaging of their software in an effort to use their company name to help their brands. When you are looking for software, you will find Microsoft Word, Microsoft Excel, or Microsoft Office, but something different happens to Microsoft that does not happen to many other company names. Consumers act like the company name is not even there! How many times have you been asked if you are proficient in some computer programs or if you are familiar with PCs and you answer with just Word, Excel or Office? Microsoft can get by with this because consumers have done the work for them. Instead of having cumbersome brand names, consumers have shortened them to easily recognizable and memorable brand names: Word, Excel, and Office.

Daniel Ayodele

13

Beware of Subbranding

Trying to build upon your brand by launching sub brands can be a tricky proposition as the fact that consumers are buying your brand does not mean they are looking for more options from it. For example, Best Western Hotels have different classes of hotels, yet the name Best Western is displayed prominently on all of them. The problem with this is that, having become successful on the idea of a good hotel at a reasonable price (a best-valued hotel), the company has to deal with the challenge of having to change the view of consumers who might think that they are paying too much to stay at a Best Western when actually they are staying at a luxury Best Western.

The category that has used sub-branding the most is the auto industry. Just by watching television you are bound to notice the plethora of available models from all the car manufacturers, foreign and domestic. This was one of the problems that led to the failure of the three big automakers in the United States. Consumers no longer equated the names Ford, Chevrolet, or Chrysler with the products with so many options to choose from and have shifted their focus to the models instead. And as we know, extending the brand hurts the company and the brand in the long run. Things got so bad for the automakers that General Motors and Chrysler had to be bailed out by the government to stay in business. One of the first things that they did was to cut production on automobiles so there are fewer choices thereby giving their brand more value.

The experience of the automakers is not to say that

all sub-branding attempts have led to poor results for companies. Many high-end companies have had success introducing low-priced sub brands that have attracted consumers that could not afford their high-end brands. Companies like Ralph Lauren and Waterford Crystal are a case in point. They have been successful with the introduction of more affordable sub brands while being able to maintain their high-end status without hurting the main brand. However, companies like these are the exception to the rule. Therefore, if your company decides to go this route, be sure to do so thoughtfully and do not overdo it. Remember that it has to be the consumer that comes first in your decision making and that sub-branding is, first and foremost, a company decision, and not a consumer one. Be careful.

14

Can You Ever Extend the Brand?

Based on what you have been reading, you could well be under the impression that you should never expand your brand while being worried that you will be stuck selling the same item for eternity. You will be happy to know that this is not the case. You can expand your brand provided you do so properly and keep all the brands in the same family or under the same umbrella.

To be successful when creating a second brand under the same company umbrella, you must give the new brands an identity of their own. Even though the brands will be under the control of your company, they must seem as though they are different and must act independent of it. Take Darden Restaurants as an example. They first opened Red Lobster in 1968 and when they wanted to introduce a second brand under their company umbrella, they did not open a restaurant called Red Lobster 2 or Red Lobster Livestock, instead they gave their restaurants entirely different names and themes. Darden Restaurants now has 1,800 restaurants that serve over 180,000 customers per year. Their restaurants include Red Lobster, Olive Garden, The Capital Grille, Bahama Breeze and Seasons 52. Chances are you have eaten at more than one of these establishments and did not know they were owned by the same parent company.

Again, this is what did the three big automakers in. Originally, the various makes or brands from General Motors, Chevrolet, Buick, Pontiac, Cadillac, and Oldsmobile were all distinguishable from one another. For General Motors, as for the others, with time, the numerous makes and models started to look so similar that consumers could not differentiate them and as a result interest in what the company had to offer waned. Before General Motors realized what they were doing to their brand, it was too late.

On their part, Japanese automakers were smart and chose a different strategy. Nissan and Toyota both released new brands of luxury automobiles but were adept enough not to call them Nissan Plus or Toyota Prime. They called their new brands Infiniti and Lexus respectively. This separated the luxury brands from what most consumers see as Nissan and Toyota automobile companies known for selling moderately priced cars and trucks, but this was done under the respective company's umbrella.

When you make the decision to introduce another brand under your company's umbrella, there are steps that you can take to succeed:

First, make sure that you keep it simple. Whatever category your product is in, stay in the same category and build upon the success that you have already recorded.

Second, pick one attribute for the new brand and stick with it. Look back at Darden Restaurants. All they did was change the theme and they are still in the restaurant business with their restaurants catering to the same market with minimal price differences.

Third, make sure that the new brand is distinctive and can stand alone.

Fourth, make sure that the parent company maintains control over any new brands introduced into the market. This will forestall any potential rivalry between the parent company and the new brand with the parent company in control to make sure that the brands stay distinctive, one from the other.

15

The Importance Of the Logo

Logos come in all shapes and sizes and it is up to you to pick one that will help your brand become a leader in its category. That said, you might think that going with a logo that looks unconventional and catchy to the consumers' eye is the best way to go, but that is often not the case. Studies have shown that the most effective logos are horizontal in shape owing to how consumers read. The vast population of the world reads from top to bottom, left to right, so there is no reason to try changing this habit in a bid to get fancy.

Besides the shape of the logo, the font you choose for the brand's name is also important to its success. Anyone who has used a computer knows that there are literally hundreds of different fonts from which you can choose but, more importantly, there is a need to realize that different fonts can project different meanings about a brand. Just by switching the font, you can make your brand appear masculine, feminine, modern, or antique, just to name a few. It is up to you to know your brand inside out so you choose the proper font to convey the message that you want sent to consumers. When it comes to choosing the font for your logo, make sure that you choose something legible. You do not want to make your brand impossible to read for consumers looking for it on the package just because you tried to "impress".

As a matter of preference, you may choose to use a symbol to signify your brand in favor of a name. A good example of a company that uses a shape to signify its brand is Nike. Nike's swoosh logo has become synonymous with the best sports equipment that consumers can buy. Many times, Nike even leaves its name off its products and all you see is the swoosh logo. However, Nike is the exception to the rule; there are not many companies that have succeeded in using only a symbol for a logo. Perhaps the only other company that has this type of success is Apple. The name Apple does not appear on the back of the iPad, iPod, or iPhone. There is just their logo, which is an apple. In this case, the logo and the company name are the same, holding a double meaning for the consumer.

The next time you go to your local mall or large shopping center, take the time to look at the logos of the stores. You will notice that the vast majority of them are horizontal and easy to read. Only a few stores have opted to use something different from the horizontal, easy-to-read option. Perhaps the most well-known company to employ this less-used format is Lord and Taylor. The company uses a script style font which makes it hard to read their name.

16

The Importance of Color

Branding

Beyond having a logo that is attractive and easy to read for consumers, you have to decide what the color of the packaging will be. This is another way for your brand to stand out against the competition, so choose wisely as colors can portray different meanings for your brand in the same way that fonts can. For instance, red is a striking color that comes across as bold and fierce while blue can be interpreted as serene and soothing.

One of the most common practices of companies when choosing a color for their packaging is to choose the color directly opposite that of their closest competitor. Just take a look at Coca Cola and Pepsi. Coca Cola is red; Pepsi is blue — directly opposite colors. Some companies are also so identified with a color such that consumers know what the product is just by seeing it. Ask anyone what the little blue box signifies and they will automatically tell you Tiffany's. If you show a picture of yellow arches to consumers, they will instantly associate it with McDonald's, even without seeing the rest of the sign. Another example of a company in this regard is UPS. They have even incorporated their color into their advertising with the slogan "What can Brown do for you?" These are companies that have been able to make their brand synonymous with just one color.

Other companies choose to use multiple colors in their logos. Companies like eBay, Google, and Microsoft have all done this. For eBay and Google, they have chosen to give each letter a different color and this sets Google apart from its closest competitor, Yahoo, which uses the color purple in its logo. In a fresh twist to this, Google has even gone to the length of letting its employees play around with their logo at certain times during the year. At holidays, significant historical events, or when it is a famous person's birthday, people who go to Google's website to use their search engine will see a variation of the original logo into something celebrating the event. This is almost unheard of with company logos, but Google, being a web-based company, uses it to set themselves apart from other companies. This has actually been shown to increase traffic to their site on important occasions because people want to see what they did with the logo.

When you decide on the color to use for your brand, make sure you use a color that is complementary. If you are trying to sell a new brand of razor blades, you probably should stay away from the color red since it might conjure up thoughts of consumers cutting themselves and bleeding. You don't want that. You would be better off choosing a color that puts the consumer at ease, like blue, especially considering that it goes with water which consumers use when they shave. This way you connect your brand with the feeling of ease in the mind of consumers who buy or use your product.

Branding

17

Think Globally

There is a limited amount of space for your brand to grow in your home country. Do not fall into the trap of expanding because your brand has reached a plateau in its category locally like many brands do. Think bigger than your home country; think globally. As a consumer, how often has the word "imported" made you take a second look at a brand? This happens so much that many countries are known for certain products. Are Swiss watches not seen as the best or Japanese automobiles as more reliable? Does the best wine not come from France and beer from Germany? These beliefs and thoughts about countries and products may not necessarily be true, but majority of consumers agree with them. However, the same consumers would think the total opposite if you were trying to sell cars from El Salvador, wine from Zimbabwe, watches from Mongolia, or beer from Fiji. The fact that these countries have no history of producing quality products would make the consumers look at the products as inferior and they would likely stay away from them.

To be successful in the global market, there are things you need to know. Ideally, your brand should be the first in its category to go global so you can have the advantages of being first in the category globally as you did in your home country. You also want your brand to fit into the needs of the countries into which you intend to expand. This will take some time and research on your part so it behooves you to get started right away, once you know that your brand is a hit in your home country. If you are a company that makes winter clothing, you will not be successful if you try to expand into Jamaica. Not a good fit.

Thinking globally when coming up with a name for your brand or product prepares you to better take advantage of the business opportunities in the global space. English is the second, most widely-used language across the globe so it is best to use it for your product and logo – most people speak Chinese but most of them are in China. In doing this, it is very important to avoid choosing a name that means one thing in English but has another meaning or connotation that could be taken as offensive in the country into which you are expanding. The practice of giving brands and products English names has already been adopted by countries that do not even speak the language as their mother tongue. Diesel Jeans come from Italy and Red Bull, which sounds like an all-American beverage, comes from Austria.

Daniel Ayodele

18

Branding and the Internet

When you make up your mind to introduce a new brand in the marketplace, you have to decide whether it is going to be strictly an online brand or a brick-and-mortar brand. Furthermore, to make your mark on the Internet, you have to follow some of the same principles that would make your brand successful in the real world. Be the first to do something and create your own category. This will make your brand the leader and authority. Take YouTube for example. They have become the leader in the category of streaming videos of all kinds on the Internet. This is an example of a web-based brand that has used the Internet to its advantage. Amazon is another company that is a web-based brand and they also dominate their category, having become the leading seller of books on the Internet, far outpacing brick-and-mortar stores like Barnes & Noble and Boarders which also have a presence online to sell books.

If you are thinking about starting a brand on the Internet, you need to ask yourself if your product or service will work online. This is important because not everything does. You also have to decide on how you want to use the Internet. Are you going to use it as a home for your business or as a platform through which consumers can reach you besides your physical location(s)? You will not be able to dominate both. Let's go back to the Amazon and Barnes & Noble example. Barnes & Noble is the most successful brick-and-mortar bookstore, far outselling its competitors. Yet, on the Internet, it does not even come close to the same sales as Amazon. Amazon concentrated on being an

Internet brand and dominates its category.

To help you decide if the Internet should be used as a place where you can start a brand or as a secondary means for customers to reach you, here are a few tips that you can explore: First, think about what your brand is. Is it something that you can hold in your hand or is it something intangible? If your brand is something that consumers can touch or hold in their hand, then it is probably best that you use the Internet as a secondary source for consumers to get your brand. If your brand is something intangible, on the other hand, perhaps a service-based company like an insurance company or a travel agency, then Internet branding is the way to go. Esurance has succeeded by only offering insurance online and sites like Expedia and Travelocity have done well by offering discounts on travel.

Second, ask yourself questions about the brand. Is the brand something that could be considered trendy or stylish? If so, then it would be best for you to use the Internet as a secondary means for consumers to reach your brand. You will find that a lot of clothing stores have websites online where consumers can buy their clothes but the vast majority of their income comes from their brick-and-mortar stores. If your brand is not considered trendy or stylish, being an Internet brand will be the best for you. Examples of brands that are not considered trendy or stylish would be those that deal with sporting equipment, computers and books. These items can easily become Internet brands and can be sold exclusively online.

Third, think about how much diversity there is with the brand. If the brand is available in countless varieties, then

Internet branding is right for it. Again, this goes back to the example of Amazon and Barnes & Noble. With Barnes & Noble being primarily a brick-and-mortar store, there is no way they can keep the same amount of books in stock as Amazon can. This limitation gives the latter the advantage to keep more obscure books available for consumers who will not be able to find them at Barnes & Noble and directly affects the number of options that brick-and-mortar stores can offer customers as they have a lot less space to hold inventory and can only stock products that sell if they want to be successful.

Fourth, ask yourself if the cost of the brand is a major reason why consumers buy the product. If the brand is more likely to be purchased because the price is low then the Internet is probably the best way to go. The main reason for this is that there are sites on the Internet which allow consumers to instantly compare the prices of goods and services across many websites at once. One advantage that online businesses have over their brick-and-mortar counterparts is that there is no tax on the Internet. This might not seem like a big deal, but the bigger the purchase the more money the consumers save and the more motivation they have to make return purchases. In addition, when consumers are able to save any amount of money they feel like they have won something. This can make purchasing a brand at a low price feel even better.

Last, if you are thinking about starting an Internet brand, you must consider shipping costs. If your proposed Internet brand will incur expensive shipping costs when a consumer purchases your brand, it is probably not a good idea to focus on the web; stay with the brick-and-mortar concept instead. However, if your Internet brand is subtle like Esurance, Expedia, or Travelocity, your shipping costs will be minimal. Most of your customers will even bear the cost of printing out all the paperwork that they will need using their personal computers at home. The biggest thing you have to ship – if that is what the consumer requests – is paperwork and that is a lot cheaper than products and brands that have weight to them.

Branding

19
Naming And The Internet

When it comes to the Internet, picking a good name is more important than picking a good name in the actual world. This is because, on the Internet, your name serves as the main reason consumers go to your site. Knowing this, you should stay away from picking a name that sounds too generic. If generic names were the way to go Buy.com would be much bigger than Amazon.com and CheapTickets.com would be bigger than Expedia and Travelocity. Therefore, follow the steps below to come up with a name that will give your Internet brand the best chance at succeeding.

First, keep the name short and simple. This makes it easier for consumers to remember as well as type it quickly and easily into their browser. Keeping the name simple and easy-to-spell is the key to success on the Internet since a consumer has to type it correctly to reach your website. One little mistake and they will be sent to a completely different site. If your brand is better known to consumers by a nickname, keep that in mind when coming up with a name for the Internet. Many companies which have been around for a while have used this to their advantage. Consumers used FedEx rather than Federal Express so much that the company changed its name to FedEx. When was the last time someone asked you if you wanted to go to Kentucky Fried Chicken? The name does not appear on their signs anymore; it has been changed to KFC. KFC.com is much easier and simpler to spell than Kentuckyfriedchicken.com.

Second, the name you choose should be distinctive. This will make your brand more memorable to consumers.

Again, stay away from the use of the generic and make sure that the name you choose implies the category that you are in. If you want to sell dog food on the Internet, do not go with a generic names like Dogfood.com. Think of something more dynamic which consumers will remember like Planetdog-food.com or Dogfooddepot.com. These names are more interesting and will be more memorable to consumers than the generic alternative. The name you choose should also conjure up a picture in the minds of consumers when they hear it. Go back to the example of the dog food. Which name brings up a more interesting picture in your mind? Is it the generic-sounding Dogfood.com or the more interesting Planet-dogfood.com and Dogfooddepot.com? Not only will the latter names create a more interesting picture in the minds of consumers, they will also help the company that has these websites in advertising and in the designing of the website. All around, they offer many more options than something plain and lifeless.

Also, you should be able to speak the name you choose. You may think that sounds silly, but just think about all the websites that are out there with initials as addresses. This makes their websites infinitely harder to remember compared to those with names that can be easily spoken, bringing up another point on naming for the Internet: mixing numbers with names. While using numbers for words makes texting faster and easier, it does not work for naming a brand or business on the Internet. If you start a website with the name Good4you.com, you will either need to have an advertising campaign to tell prospective consumers how to spell your name or you will have to pay the extra expense of owning two domain names, Good4you.com and Goodforyou.com. This is a cost that you do not need to incur. Why pick a confusing name only to spend more money? Besides, names composed of a mixture of numbers and letters are much harder to remember than those comprising just letters or numbers. So, pick one and stick with it.

Branding

20

Globalization and the Internet

Perhaps no other medium has more affect on the global economy than the Internet. As a platform that is accessible from all parts of the world, it has broken down barriers that have long stood in the way of doing business on a global scale. Today, a small company in a rural part of the country can do business with anyone, anywhere in the world. This is an exciting option when starting an Internet brand.

The advantages offered through the internet when doing business on a global scale is an important factor to consider when having your website designed. Have the website designed such that its contents can be translated into several different languages. This will help your brand become global. Some companies are already reaping the benefits of the globalization available through the Internet. Amazon, although based in the United States, is the largest seller of books in the United Kingdom and more than twenty percent of its sales comes from purchases made outside the United States.

Some Internet businesses choose not to allow the option to translate the content on their website to other languages, choosing to go with the English-only option. Those companies choose to do this because they think that going with the English-only option gives their website a more exclusive and luxury feel. Also, they reason that since English is the second, most spoken language in the world, in addition to being used as the language of business, spending the time and money to equip their website with the capability to translate content into several languages might be a waste of money. Besides, companies located in non-English speaking countries are naming their brands in English. You have already seen the examples of Red Bull, a brand that comes from Austria, and Diesel Jeans, one that comes from Italy. These are just a couple of the products from non-English speaking countries that have been given English names.

The opportunity to go global is another reason to stay away from a generic name. If you are trying to sell shoes on the Internet, naming the site Shoes.com is akin to shooting yourself in the foot. The word "shoes" does not mean the same thing in all languages so non-English speaking people will have no idea what you are selling and will not go to your site. This is why Nike is successful. If they had called their company Athletic Gear, they would not have had the success that they now enjoy. Nike means the same thing to consumers across the globe. Athletic teams across the world wear Nike gear so, when consumers are looking to buy some athletic equipment on the Internet, typing the word Nike into the computer is an easy thing to do and it is the first name that comes to their mind when they want to purchase athletic gear.

Conclusion

As you have read, a lot goes into making a brand successful. However, do not let the steps intimidate you or cause you to second-guess your goals for you will be able to bring a new brand to the market and make it a success as long as you take the time to make informed decisions and remember to think like a consumer through the process. While that is not an easy thing to do when you are excited about your brand and seek to make your company a success, it is important to be mindful of the fact that it is the consumer who buys the brand, the company only makes it.

As a COMPANY, you have to make the brand or product the best it can be and you are in complete control of that part of your business. You even get to influence the image you want the brand to conjure up as well as the message you send out to consumers. However, it is consumers who have the last word on whether or not your brand becomes a success. This is why it is very important to make sure that you hold focus groups and do surveys to get feedback directly from the potential customers of your brand.

• • •

By FOLLOWING the steps that you have read, you will be able to build a brand that is a leader in the category of your choosing, one that consumers will desire to identify with and seek out at the local stores for the promised satisfaction that they made the best decision they could have made for themselves and their family when they purchased your product. When people feel this way about a product, they are bound to become repeat customers, giving you a sustainable market for years to come while jumpstarting your brand to garner the largest market share in its home country and to secure the best chance at expanding into the global market. Do not forget that it is almost impossible for your brand to be replaced when it reaches a leadership position.

Daniel Ayodele

Branding

www.ingramcontent.com/pod-product-compliance
Lightning Source LLC
Chambersburg PA
CBHW040321220526
45473CB00009B/2519